The Diabetes Fix:

How to escape and reverse type 2 diabetes

By

Dr. Kory maggio

Copyright © by Dr. Kory Maggio 2023 all rights reserved.

Before this document is duplicated or reproduced in any manner, the publisher's consent must be gained. Therefore the content within can neither be stored electronically, transferred, nor kept in a database. Neither in part nor full can the document be copied, scanned, faxed, or retained without approval from the publisher or creator.

TABLE OF CONTE

INTRODUCTION
PREVENTING TYPE 2 DIABETES
CHAPTER 1
What is the distinction among type 1 and type 2 diabetes
CHAPTER 2
How to reverse and avoid type 2 diabetes
CHAPTER 3
Sucrose and the danger of type 2 diabetes
CHAPTER 4
Diabetes treatment
CHAPTER 5
Carbohydrate-reduced Diet
Conclusion

INTRODUCTION

PREVENTING TYPE 2 DIABETES

Perhaps you have heard that you have a high probability of having type 2 diabetes, the most widespread sort of diabetes. You could be fat or have a parent, brother, or sister with type 2 diabetes. Perhaps you had childbearing diabetes, which is diabetes that develops during pregnancy. These are just a few examples of factors that can enhance your risk of developing type 2 diabetes.

Diabetes can cause major health complications, such as heart disease, stroke, and vision and foot troubles. Prediabetes could also generate health complications. The positive news is that type 2 diabetes can be postponed or perhaps averted. The longer you have diabetes, the more likely you are to acquire health problems; hence, postponing diabetes by even a few years will benefit your health. You may help prevent or procrastinate type 2 diabetes by losing a modest amount of weight by

Following a reduced-calorie eating plan and being physically active most days of the week.

How can I lower my odds of having type 2 diabetes?

Here are some things you can adjust to lessen your risk:

Lose weight and keep it off. You might be able to obstruct or delay diabetes by losing 5 to 7 percent of your beginning weight. 1 For instance, if you weigh 200 pounds, your target would be to lose around 10 to 14 pounds.

Move more. Get at minimal 30 minutes of physical exercise five days a week. If you have not been active, consult with your health care physician about which activities are optimal. Start cautiously to build up to your goal.

Eat healthful foods most of the time. Eat smaller quantities to limit the amount of calories you eat each day and help you lose weight. Choosing foods with less fat is another technique to limit calories. Drink water instead of sugary beverages.

Most often, your greatest chance of preventing type 2 diabetes is to establish lifestyle changes that work for you long-term. Get started with preventing type 2 diabetes.

About 1 in 3 Americans has prediabetes, according to research from the Centers for Disease Control and Prevention. You will not know if you have prediabetes except you are tested.
If you have prediabetes, you can lessen your likelihood of having type 2 diabetes. Forget weight if you demand to, become more physically active, and follow a reduced-calorie eating plan.

In this book, you will learn the basic methods and tips to avoid and treat diabetes for life. Sit, relax, and stay tuned for these life-transforming techniques.

CHAPTER 1

What is the distinction among type 1 and type 2 diabetes

Most people know there are two types of diabetes, but not everyone understands the distinction between them.
In both type 1 and type 2 diabetes, blood sugar levels can get too high because the body doesn't generate insulin (a hormone that regulates blood sugar) or does not utilize insulin correctly. Though the illness is fundamentally the same in both kinds, they have different causes and cures.

Here's everything you need to know
Type one diabetes is a genetic ailment that typically shows up early in childhood, while type 2 diabetes is primarily diet-related and develops over time. If you have type 1 diabetes, your resistant system is attacking and destroying the insulin-producing cells in your pancreas.

The pancreas is the flat organ that looks kind of like an elongated sideways comma that hangs out behind your stomach.)

The good news is that today's treatments allow people with type 1 diabetes to learn to regulate the repercussions of the illness and yet live a relatively "normal" life.

There are a few techniques to treat type 1 diabetes
Monitor your blood sugar
Living with diabetes entails getting familiar with healthy blood sugar levels and checking them often.
Depending on your health care provider's precise advice, you might need to check it four to ten times daily. You'll use a small blood sugar meter called a glucometer to measure glucose levels in a pinprick of blood on a disposable test strip. An additional potential is to have a constant glucose monitor, which automatically measures your blood sugar every few minutes using a sensor inserted underneath the skin.
Take insulin
Because your body doesn't generate it on its own, you'll have to receive it in another way.

There are various strategies for taking insulin, including daily injections or a wearable insulin pump, which administers modest, regular quantities of fast-acting insulin throughout the day through a thin tube.

Though it's certainly not the most comfortable lifestyle, it often becomes second nature for people living with type 1 diabetes.

Maintain a balanced diet

You don't have to be overly restrictive, but carbohydrates are the meals you'll want to watch, making sure to eat them consistently but not go overboard. If you're taking a precise dosage of insulin, keeping your carbohydrate consumption consistent is crucial.

Exercise

Staying active is always a crucial component of health, but for individuals with type 1 diabetes, it can help maintain blood sugar levels in check and cause your body to utilize insulin more efficiently.

What are the indications of type 1 diabetes

If you or a loved one display these symptoms, it's worth getting checked out:

.Increased thirst
.Frequent urination Unexplained weight loss. Fatigue and weakness Blurred vision.

Diagnosing type 1 diabetes

To diagnose type 1 diabetes, you will have to get blood tests done, one of which is called an A1C screening. A1C scans analyze your blood sugar levels from the past two to three months and can be used to detect type 1 diabetes, type 2 diabetes, and prediabetes.
Life line screening also offers an A1C screening at the convenience of your own home through our home tests.

When it becomes an emergency

There's a complication of type 1 diabetes called diabetic ketoacidosis (DKA), which occurs with very high blood sugar and is serious and life-threatening. With DKA, the cells in the body are starved for energy, so they start breaking down fat, producing deadly compounds known as ketones. So if you or someone you know gets these symptoms on top of diabetes symptoms, it's time to hurry and get treatment:

.Nausea and vomiting
.Severe abdominal pain
.chest pain. Coma.
The diagnosis of DKA most typically follows a diagnosis of type 1 diabetes.

Another worry is low blood sugar, or hypoglycemia, which could arise from taking too much insulin.

Hypoglycemia needs therapy straight away to get the blood sugar back to normal—usually with high-sugar foods, drinking juice or conventional soft beverages, eating candy, or taking glucose tablets or gel.

If blood sugar levels drop too low, indications and symptoms can include:
.Fatigue
.Pale skin
.Shakiness
.An irregular or fast heartbeat
.Anxiety

.Sweating
.Hunge
.Irritability
.Tingling or coldness of the lips, lingua or cheek

Type 2 diabetes

Type 2 diabetes is more frequent in the U.S. than type 1, and it is mostly caused by lifestyle.

With type 2 diabetes, your body still makes a limited quantity of insulin, but it isn't effective enough. The pancreas can't keep up with the high blood sugar levels originating from improper food and a lack of exercise. Some patients with type 2 diabetes genuinely have "insulin resistance," which means the pancreas creates insulin but the body does not recognize it (this is separate from type 1, in which the insulin-producing cells are being assaulted by the immune system).

Type 2 diabetes risk factors

Your probability of acquiring type 2 diabetes is enhanced if your diet is high in carbs and fat but low in fiber, if you're not very physically active, and/or if you have high blood pressure.

High alcohol usage and age are other risk factors. Though genes can play a component in the chance of having type 2 diabetes, it can be prevented with the appropriate lifestyle choices, unlike type 1.

How to treat type 2 diabetes

Unlike patients with type 1, patients with type 2 diabetes often do not need to take insulin because their bodies still make a modest amount of it.

Though there are medicines like Metformin available to assist in decreasing blood sugar, **the basic ways to manage type 2 diabetes include**

A balanced diet Eating fruits and vegetables, complete grains, and lean meats while avoiding more than the occasional high-fat, high-sugar dish is the first and most crucial step to controlling type 2 diabetes.

Exercise Staying active is also very important. There are so many strategies for acquiring exercise. Try different activities to locate a form of exercise you enjoy and integrate it into your weekly schedule.

Weight loss of course, if you work toward eating healthier and exercising more, this may be positive. Losing weight is less about the number on the scale and more about taking care of your body and lowering the pressure on your pancreas.

Blood glucose monitoring Checking your blood sugar routinely will become a part of your everyday routine.

It's vital to stay up-to-date on how your levels are going throughout the day and modify your meals and activities accordingly. After a while, you'll discover the program and balance that work best for you.

How can I tell if I have type 2 diabetes

If you are experiencing the symptoms below, it's a good idea to be checked out:

.Excessive thirst

.Frequent urination

.Tingling or numbness in your hands or feet

.Fatigue

.Blurry vision Increased hunger
.Itchy skin.

Prevention
Because of the genetic root of type 1 diabetes, blood tests to determine the likelihood of type 1 aren't done regularly or encouraged by clinicians. When symptoms do appear, blood testing is necessary for diagnosis. As previously discussed, an A1C examination analyzes blood sugar levels from the past two to three months and is typically utilized for the diagnosis of type 1, type 2, and prediabetes.

In contrast, there are various measures to lower your risk of type 2 diabetes. It's particularly critical if you have a history of diabetes in your family.

Ways to lessen your risk include
.Exercise and weight management.
.Healthy diet.
.Maintain typical blood pressure.
.Maintain minimal alcohol consumption.
.Quit smoking.

.Increase your fiber intake.

Prediabetes suggests you have a higher than typical blood sugar level, but it's not high enough to be declared type 2 diabetes yet. The causes, signs, and preventions are basically the same as for type 2, but those under 45 have a substantially lower risk.

If you encounter any of the signs of diabetes or prediabetes, be careful to be tested as soon as you can. Schedule an A1C screening to get started.

The bottom line

Type 1 diabetes is a historical illness that often shows up early in life, but type 2 diabetes is established over time, largely due to food.

In both instances, your body does not make enough insulin to effectively maintain your blood sugar, but for different reasons. If you're experiencing symptoms, you can get tested for diabetes with an A1C screening, which measures your blood sugar for the past 2–3 months.

CHAPTER 2

How to reverse and avoid type 2 diabetes

Type two diabetes is a chronic medical illness that affect millions of people worldwide.

Unmanaged diabetes may lead to blindness, renal failure, heart disease, and other devastating conditions.

Before examination your blood sugar levels may raise but not high enough to indicate diabetes. This is called prediabetes. Taking a test like this one from a trusted source will help you figure out your risk factors for this condition.

It is foreknown that up to 37% of patients with untreated prediabetes will develop type 2 diabetes within 4 years.

The Diabetes Fix

Here are eight techniques to lower your probability of acquiring diabetes:

1 Reduce your total carb intake

The quantity and quality of your carb intake are both critical variables to consider when making dietary alterations to help prevent diabetes.

Your body decompose carbs into tiny sugar particles, which are absorbed into your bloodstream. The accompanying spike in blood sugar stimulates your pancreas to manufacture insulin, a hormone that helps sugar pass from your bloodstream into your cells.

In patients with prediabetes, the body's cells are resistant to insulin; hence, blood sugar remains high.

To compensate, the pancreas generates extra insulin, seeking to bring blood sugar down.

Over time, this can lead to steadily rising blood sugar and insulin levels until the illness develops into type 2 diabetes.

Many studies link frequent added sugar or refined carb intake with diabetes risk.

What's more, replacing these things with foods that have less of an effect on blood sugar may lower your risk. However, all food sources — not only sugar and processed carbs—increase the release of insulin. Although refined carbs are digested more promptly than complex carbs, there's inconsistent evidence indicating a food's blood sugar surge is related to diabetes risk. Therefore, managing overall carb intake and choosing carbs that are high in fiber are likely better ways to prevent diabetes than just reducing highly processed carbs.

Examples of meals and drinks high in added sugars or refined carbs include

Soda, candy, dessert, white bread, spaghetti, and sweetened breakfast cereal.

Non-starchy veggies like broccoli and mushrooms, whole fruit, oats, and whole grain bread and pasta are better substitutes. These selections are higher in fiber, which helps limit spikes in blood sugar.

Lean proteins like fish and healthy fats like olive oil, avocado, almonds, and seeds also have less of an effect on blood sugar. They're wonderful additions to your diet to help avoid type 2 diabetes.

2 Exercise regularly

Doing physical activity consistently may help prevent diabetes.

People with prediabetes often have poor insulin sensitivity, also known as insulin resistance. In this scenario, your pancreas has to make more insulin to get sugar out of your blood and into your cells.

Exercise enhances the insulin sensitivity of your cells, suggesting that you require less insulin to maintain your blood sugar levels.

Many types of physical activity have been found to improve insulin resistance and blood sugar in patients with prediabetes or type 2 diabetes.

These involve high impact work out, high-concentration interval training, and strength training.

One study in 29 adults with type 2 diabetes indicated that, which involves bursts of intensive activity followed by brief recoveries, led to improved blood sugar management and longer sessions of endurance training.

However, you don't need to exercise for long to obtain benefits. Short exercise bouts that last as little as 10 minutes, such as brisk walking, are fantastic possibilities. If you're just beginning an exercise routine, start with quick workouts and work up to 150 minutes per week.

3 Drink water as your principal beverage

Sticking with water as your drink of choice will help you limit beverages that are heavy in sugar.

Sugary beverages, including soda and sweetened fruit juice, have been connected to an elevated incidence of both type 2 diabetes and latent autoimmune diabetes in adults (LADA).

One large observational study of 2,800 individuals found that those who drank more than 2 glasses of sugary beverages per day had a 99% and 20% higher risk of LADA and type 2 diabetes, respectively.

In addition, research found that 1 serving of sugar-sweetened drinks per day may elevate the prevalence of type 2 diabetes by 18%.

In contrast, increasing water intake may contribute to better blood sugar management and insulin response. One 24-week experiment found that adults who replaced diet drinks with water while following a weight loss program exhibited a decrease in insulin resistance, fasting blood sugar, and insulin levels.

4 Try to decrease the extra weight

Carrying excess weight may increase your risk of type 2 diabetes.

In particular, visceral fat—excess weight in your stomach and around your abdominal organs — is related to insulin resistance, inflammation, prediabetes, and type 2 diabetes. Notably, decreasing even a minor amount of weight — as little as 5–7%—may help lessen your risk of type 2 diabetes.

A randomized, 2-year trial in more than 1,000 patients at increased risk of type 2 diabetes found that exercise, nutrition, and weight loss therapies drastically cut the incidence of this disease by 40% to 47% compared with a control group.

Healthy weight-loss solutions include:
Preparing a balanced plate with non-starchy veggies, lean proteins, complex carbs, and healthy fats is a good place to start.

5 Quit smoking

Smoking has been demonstrated to cause or contribute to various serious health conditions, including heart disease, chronic obstructive pulmonary disease (COPD), and lung and intestinal cancers.

Research also connected smoking to type 2 diabetes. While the mechanics aren't totally known, it's suspected that smoking may cause insulin resistance and impede insulin secretion.

Plus, heavy, more frequent smoking is associated with a higher risk of diabetes than smoking fewer cigarettes.

Importantly, data suggest that stopping smoking may reduce diabetes risk.

One significant study in more than 53,000 Japanese participants suggested that diabetes risk in those who smoke diminishes over time after ceasing.

Smoking cessation for 10 or more years may even decrease this risk to virtually the same level as for people who never smoked.

6 Reduce your portion sizes

Eating portion sizes suitable for your needs may also help prevent diabetes.

Eating too much food at one time has been proven to generate elevated blood sugar and insulin levels in people at risk of diabetes. Smaller amounts may lead to reduced calorie consumption and subsequent weight loss, which may in turn lessen your risk of diabetes. Though there are few studies on the pressure of portion management on people

With prediabetes, research on those with type 2 diabetes offers some insight.

Studies about grown-ups with fat or obesity Involves type 2 diabetes, following a meal plan with portion-managed meal replacements and appropriate portions of other healthy meals leds to weight loss and cut in body fat. Ground Rules for the prevention and control of type 2 diabetes support portion management as a way to help individuals maintain a healthy weight.

To minimize your portion proportions, make your plate half non-starchy veggies, a quarter lean protein, and a quarter complex carbs like fruit or whole grains. If you're at a restaurant that serves large amounts, consider an appetizer for your main entrée or ask for a half quantity. Plus, instead of eating snacks immediately out of the bag, pour the appropriate amount into a separate dish.

Cut back on sedentary behaviors

It's basic to avoid lazy attitude, such as obtaining very little physical activity or sitting for much of the day, to help prevent diabetes.

Observational studies consistently correlate sedentary behavior with an increased risk of type 2 diabetes.

One study in more than 6,000 older women indicated that those who had the largest amount of idle time per day — 10 or more hours — were more than twice as likely to acquire diabetes than those with 8.3 hours or less of sedentary time.

Changing lazy attitude can be as easy as standing up from your desk and walking around for a few minutes every half hour. Using a fitness watch or accessories that remembers you to walk at least 250 steps per hour may also be helpful.

Still, it could be tough to modify tightly set behavior, It is vital to create sensible and achievable goals, such as standing when conversing on the phone or taking the stairs instead of the elevator.

8 Follow a high-fiber diet.

Eating plenty of dietary fiber is important for gut health and weight management. It may also help avoid diabetes. Studies in adults with prediabetes and older women with obesity suggest that this vitamin helps keep blood sugar and insulin levels low.

Fiber can be broken into two fundamental categories:

Soluble, which absorbs water, and insoluble, which doesn't.
Soluble fiber and water form a gel in the digestive tract that slows down food absorption, resulting in a more gradual rise in blood sugar. Thus, consuming more dissolved fiber may decrease fasting blood sugar and insulin levels.

Insoluble fiber has also been connected to decreases in blood sugar levels in people with diabetes using fiber supplements instead of high-fiber diets, so gaining more fiber from meals is likely favorable.

CHAPTER 3

Sucrose and the danger of type 2 diabetes
What is type 2 diabetes?

The Diabetes Fix

Diabetes is a lifelong disorder that causes a person's blood sugar to be too high.

The are two kinds of diabetes: type 1 and type 2. Insulin is a hormone that is vital for regulating blood glucose levels. Type 2 diabetes can occur either as a result of insulin receptors getting desensitized and, as a result, no longer responding to insulin, or due to the beta cells of the pancreas no longer manufacturing insulin. Often, it is a combination of these two elements that leads to this ailment known as type 2 diabetes.

Type 2 diabetes is by far the most frequent type; Of all the individuals who have diabetes, 90% of them have type 2. Diabetes is an increasing health issue in the UK, with 3.2 million people diagnosed with the disease and a further

850,000 estimated to be undiagnosed. Diabetes is a rising health burden, and it is estimated that by 2025, 5 million people will have been diagnosed in the UK.

Diabetes is the biggest cause of blindness in the UK, and the disease's complications cause greater than 100 cut away to take place each week. Each year, 24,000 people die early from diabetes-associated complications. Its total cost is estimated at £13.8 billion each year. It is estimated that the yearly NHS cost of the direct treatment of diabetes in the UK will increase to £16.9 billion over the next 25 years, which is 17 percent of the NHS budget and is considered to potentially bankrupt the NHS.

What are the causes of type 2 diabetes?

There is a complicated combination of inherited and environmental risk factors that play a part in the development of diabetes; it tends to cluster in families, Ethnicity also plays a major role in its development, with people of South Asian descent being six times more likely to suffer from the disease.

Obesity is the major risk factor, accounting for 80–85% of the total risk of obtaining type 2 diabetes .

Given that nearly 2 in 3 people in the UK are overweight, their chances of acquiring Type 2 diabetes at some point are substantial unless they take quick action.

Other risk groups include:

People above the age of 40
People with cardiovascular disease
Women with polycystic ovarian syndrome (PCOS) People who are taking medication for schizophrenia or bipolar disorder

How can sugar add to the risk of type 2 diabetes

Type 2 diabetes occurs as a result of a deficit in insulin production or an increased resistance to insulin. Insulin is a hormone created by the pancreas that allows for the regulation of the intake of glucose. It is released in reaction to growing glucose levels in the blood and allows select cells to take up glucose from the blood to metabolize it.

A high-sugar diet has been linked to an increased incidence of type 2 diabetes due to the links between high sugar intake and obesity.

The Scientific Advisory Committee on Nutrition (SACN) has completed a meta-analysis, which contains nine cohort studies in 11 publications that suggest that there is a relationship between sugar-sweetened beverages and the incidence of type 2 diabetes. The connection between sugar consumption and diabetes is both direct and indirect, with sugar-sweetened beverages being directly associated with the prevalence of type 2 diabetes and sugar consumption leading to fat, one of the major danger cause for type 2 diabetes.

Complications related to type 2 diabetes

There are several issues related to type 2 diabetes. The most frequent are: Kidney disease
Eye disease includes blindness
Amputation
Depression
Neuropathy
Sexual dysfunction Complications in pregnancy
Dementia
Current sugar consumption and consultation on how to escape type 2 diabetes

The current suggestion for sugar intake is that it not exceed 10% of daily energy intake.

The new study published by the SACN has emphasized the need for this percentage to be further reduced to 5% (30g of sugars). The guideline for kids is 24 g/day for children aged 5–11 and 19 g/day for children aged 4-6. At present, we consume a much higher proportion of sugar each day, with percentage sugar consumption between 1.5

and 3 year olds at 11.9%, 4 to 10 year olds at 14.7%, and 11 to 18 year olds at 15.6%.

It is also vital to maintain a healthy lifestyle and nutrition by: Not exceeding the allowed number of calories per day—2,000 calories per day for women and 2,500 calories per day for males. Reducing sugar intake to a limit of 6 tablespoons per day (25g). Reducing the use of sugar-sweetened beverages. Work out for a limited time, five times a week (moderate intensity exercise). Justify body weight at a well standard (between 18.5 kg/m2 and 24.9 kg/m2).

maintaining a healthy waist-to-hip ratio, as it is a good indication of abdominal fat and subsequently diabetes.

CHAPTER 4

Diabetes treatment

Medications for type 2 diabetes

Lifestyle decisions, such as eating nutritious food, exercising, and remaining at a healthy weight, are key to managing type 2 diabetes. But you also may demand to take drugs to keep your blood sugar, often called glucose, at a healthy level. Sometimes one medicine is enough. In some cases, taking many medicines works better.

The list of medicines for type 2 diabetes is long and could be baffling. Take time to comprehend these drugs—how they're used, what they do, and what unwanted effects they may produce. That might help you get ready to talk to your health care physician about diabetes treatment choices that are right for you.

Diabetes treatment: lowering blood sugar

Several classes of type 2 diabetic medicines exist. Each form of medicine works in a different way to lower blood sugar. A medication may work by:

Causing the pancreas to create and release more insulin.

Restricting the liver's capability to build and discharge sugar blocking the activity of enzymes in the intestines that break down carbohydrates, limiting how rapidly cells take in carbohydrates.

Help cells' awearness to insulin restrictions, the kidneys' ability to take in sugar which increases the quantity of sugar that leaves the body in urine. Slowing how swiftly food moves through the stomach.

Each level of drugs has one or extra drugs. Some of these treatments are given by mouth, while others must be taken as a shot.

Compare diabetes medications

Below is a list of common diabetic medicines. Other medications are also available. Ask your health care professional about your choices and the pros and cons of each.

Medications you take by mouth
Meglitinides
Medications
Repaglinide Nateglinide

Action: Activate the discharge of insulin from the pancreas
Advantages
Work quickly
Possible side effects
Blood sugar levels drop too low, a condition termed hypoglycemia.
Weight increase

Sulfonylureas

Medications

Glipizide (Glucotrol XL)

Glimepiride (Amaryl) Glyburide (DiaBeta, Glynase)

Action

Trigger the release of insulin from the pancreas

Advantages

Low cost

Effective in reducing blood sugar

Possible side effects

Blood sugar levels drop too low.

Weight gain

Outbreak of spot, nausea, or ejecting if you take alcohol.

Dipeptidyl-peptidase 4 (DPP-4) inhibitors and medications

Saxagliptin (Onglyza)

Sitagliptin (Januvia)

Linagliptin (Tradjenta)

Alogliptin (Nesina)

Action:
Cause the discharge of insulin when clot sugar is rising. Limit the liver's ability to release glucose.

Advantages
Don't cause weight gain.
Don't cause blood sugar levels to drop too low when delivered alone or with metformin.

Possible side effects
Upper respiratory tract infection
Sore throat and headache

Biguanides
Medications

Metformin (Fortamet, Glumetza, and others)
Action
restricts the liver's capability to discharge sugar; improve cells' sensitivity to insulin.

Advantages
Very effective
May lead to minor weight loss.

Low cost

Possible side effects

Nausea

Stomach pain

Diarrhea

Very rarely, the harmful development of lactic acid — a condition termed lactic acidosis—in persons with kidney failure or liver failure

Thiazolidinediones

Medications

Rosiglitazone (Avandia)

Pioglitazone (Actos)

Action

Improve cells' sensitivity to insulin

Limit the liver's ability to generate and release sugar.

Advantages

May slightly elevate high-density lipoprotein (HDL) cholesterol, the "good" cholesterol.

Possible side effects

Weight gain

Fluid retention

Increased probability of broken bones

Increased chance of heart complications, including heart failure

Available multiple danger of bladder cancer with pioglitazone

Alpha-glucosidase inhibitors
Medications
A carbose Miglitol (Glyset)
Action

Slow the body's ability to absorb carbohydrates and certain sugars
Advantages
Don't cause weight gain.

Don't cause blood sugar levels to drop too low unless you take them with insulin or a sulfonylurea.
Possible side effects
Gas
Stomach pain

Diarrhea

Sodium-glucose transporter 2 (SGLT2) inhibitors
Medications

Canagliflozin (Invokana)
Dapagliflozin (Farxiga)

Empagliflozin (Jardiance)
Ertugliflozin (Steglatro)

Action
Limit the kidneys' ability to take in sugar, which increases the quantity of sugar that leaves the body in urine.

Advantages
May lead to a weight decrease.
May reduce blood pressure.

Possible side effects
Urinary tract infections
Yeast infections

Bile acid sequestrants
Medications
Colesevelam (Welchol)
Action

Lower cholesterol and have a small effect on reducing blood sugar when used with other diabetic medicines.

Advantages

Likely safe for individuals with liver issues.

Possible adverse effects Gas . Constipation . Indigestion . Rise in blood fats termed triglycerides. Drugs you use as a shot Amylin mimetics drugs . Pramlintide (Symlin)

Action

Help manage blood sugar.

Slow food goes through the stomach. Used with insulin injections

Advantages

May decrease hunger

May lead to minor weight loss.

Possible side effects

Blood sugar levels drop too low.

Nausea

Abdominal discomfort

Incretin mimetic (GLP-1 receptor agonists)

Medications
Dulaglutide (Trulicity)
Exenatide (Byetta, Bydureon Bcise)
Liraglutide (Saxenda, Victoza)
Lixisenatide (Adlyxin)
Semaglutide (Ozempic, Rybelsus, and Wegoby)

Action:
Cause the discharge of insulin as clot sugar levels are rising. Could be used with metformin, basal insulin, or a sulfonylurea.

Advantages
May decrease hunger
May lead to a weight decrease.

Possible side effects
Nausea
Vomiting
Diarrhea
Abdominal discomfort
Increased chance of an inflamed pancreas — a condition termed pancreatitis

How to choose your diabetes medicine
Not every diabetes treatment is best for everyone. What works for one person might not work for the other. Your health care practitioner can explain how one prescription or several medications may fit into your diabetic treatment program.

Sometimes, combining medications may increase the efficiency of each particular medicine to lower blood sugar. Talk to your doctor about the advantages and downsides of various diabetic medicines

CHAPTER 5

Carbohydrate-reduced Diet

Low-carb diets are frequently used to promote weight loss and balance blood sugar levels. Though recommendations can vary depending on your daily carb allotment, most low-carb diets frequently prohibit foods high in carbs or added sugar.

A low-carb diet decreases carbohydrates, such as those found in pasta, bread, and sweet meals. It's great in protein, lad, and greens.

There are many different sorts of low-carb diets. Studies suggest that they can produce weight loss and increase your health.

This is a complete meal plan for a low-carb diet. It specifies what to consume and what to limit. It also offers a sample low-carb menu for a week.

Low-carb eating: the essentials

Low-carb diets have been connected with many health advantages and are extensively used to promote weight loss and regulate blood sugar levels.

There are numerous sorts of low-carb diets, and they differ based on the amount of carbs allotted each day.

A typical low-carb diet usually contains less than 26% of total daily calories from carbs. For those following a 2000-calorie diet, this represents fewer than 130 grams (g) of carbs per day.

Generally, low-carb diets limit meals heavy in carbohydrates or added sugar, including sweets, starches, and refined grains.

However, the products you're permitted to eat on a low-carb diet can change depending on your daily carb allotment. Even higher-carb meals like fruits, starchy grees and whole grains can fit into some low-carb diets in moderation.

Here is a sample of the most popular low-carb eating patterns:

Ketogenic (keto) diet: This low-carb, high-fat dietary pattern limits daily carb intake to less than 10% of total calories, or around 20–50 g of carbs.

In addition to restricting your carb intake, the keto diet also advocates ingesting high-fat goods, including avocados, olive oil, full-fat dairy products, and coconut oil.

Atkins diet: This low-carb, high-protein diet is generally separated into multiple stages, which vary in terms of your daily carb limit. During the initial phase of the Atkins diet, carb intake is limited to 20–40 g per day, depending on which plan you choose.

Over the course of the diet, your intake slowly increases but generally doesn't surpass 100 g per day.

South Beach diet: In addition to limiting carb intake, the South Beach diet encourages lean proteins and heart-healthy fats. During the initial period, grains and fruits are also off-limits. However, these foods are progressively brought back into the diet over the second and third phases of the regimen.

Paleo diet: Designed to mirror the eating patterns of our hunter-gatherer ancestors, the Paleo diet supports foods including meats, fruits, and vegetables.

The paleo diet isn't designed to be a low-carb diet, but it's naturally low in carbs as it avoids numerous carb-rich items, including grains, legumes, and dairy products.

Dukan diet: The Dukan diet is a stringent, low-carb diet that's high in protein and low in fat.
It encourages "pure protein," like lean meats. It's separated into four phases designed to assist you in attaining your weight loss goals.

Foods to eat

A low-carb diet should include a range of minimally processed, low-carb foods, including protein sources, non-starchy veggies, and high-fat dairy items.

Here are some of the meals to eat on a low-carb diet:
Meat: beef, lamb, pork, chicken
Fish: salmon, trout, haddock, and tuna
Eggs: entire eggs, egg whites, egg yolks
Non-starchy vegetables: spinach, broccoli, cauliflower, carrots, asparagus, and tomatoes
Lower-carb fruits: oranges, blueberries, strawberries, raspberries, and blackberries
Nuts and seeds: almonds, walnuts, sunflower seeds, chia seeds, and pistachios
High-butter dairy: mallow, margarine, bulk cream, Greek yogurt
Lard and oils: lard avocados, avocado oil, olive oil, coconut oil

If you are attempting to reach or maintain a reasonable weight, limit your intake of higher-calorie foods like cheese and almonds. It's easy to overdo them.

Foods to include in moderation
Unless you're following an extremely low-carb or keto diet, you may also wish to incorporate tiny amounts of the foods listed below:
Starchy grains: potatoes, sweet tuber, yams, peas, corn
Higher-carb fruits: bananas, pineapples, mangoes, and many more.
Whole grains: brown rice, and oats
Legumes: lentils, black beans, pinto beans, chickpeas

Higher-carb dairy: milk and full-fat yogurt
What's more, you can take the following reasonable if you want.
Dark chocolate with at least 70% cocoa
Dry wines with no added sugar or carbohydrates,
Dark chocolate is abundant in antioxidants and may provide health advantages if you eat it in moderation.

However, be warned that both dark chocolate and alcohol may affect weight management if you consume or drink too much.

Beverages

In addition to examining what you're placing on your plate, it's also crucial to examine what you're drinking while following a low-carb diet.

Because many beverages can be high in carbs and calories, it's preferable to choose drinks that are free of added sugar wherever feasible.

A few examples of low-carb beverages include:
coffee, tea, and water
sugar-free carbonated beverages, including sparkling water

Foods to limit

Foods heavy in added sugar and carbs should be savored only rarely on a low-carb diet.

Depending on your daily carb intake, you might need to limit or avoid the following foods:

Sweet snacks: candy, ice cream, baked goods, various things that have added sugar

Captivated seeds: white rice, white spaghetti, tortillas, and crackers

Meals and low-fat items: involves dairy yield, cereals, or crackers that are low in fat yet have added sugar

Highly processed foods: convenience meals, fast food, cookies, chips, and pretzels

Sugar-enhanced drinks: soda, sweet beverage, sports drinks, and energy drinks

Be sure to check the ingredient list of items to locate selections that fit into your diet.

Sample low-carb meal plan

This is a sample menu for a week on a low-carb diet plan. Before starting a low-carb meal, you must consult with a doctor or dietitian to identify a carbohydrate intake that works for you, depending on your health goals and personal preferences.

You can vary the amount of carbs in any of the sample meals shown below by altering the portion sizes or introducing additional snacks as needed.

Monday
Breakfast: 2 pieces of sprouted Ezekiel bread with 1/2 avocado, salt, and pepper. Total carbs: 36.5 g

Lunch: 3 ounces (85 g) of grilled chicken with 2 cups (340 g) of zucchini noodles cooked with 1 clove of garlic butter, and 1 ounce (28 g) of Parmesan. Total carbs: 17 g

Dinner: a bunless burger with a portion of Cheddar cheese, served with 1/2 cup (78 g) cooked broccoli and 2 tablespoons (35.7 g) of salsa. Total carbs: 8.5 g
Total carbohydrates for the day: 62 g

Tuesday
Breakfast: 7 oz (200 g) Transparent Greek yogurt with 1/4 cup (37 g) blueberries and 1 oz (28.35 g) almonds. Total carbs: 19.4 g
Lunch: 3 oz (85 g) rib eye barbeque and 1/2 cup (120 g) mashed rutabaga and 1 cup (129 g) sautéed green beans. Total carbs: 13.5 g
Dinner: 3 oz (85 g) baked salmon with 1/2 cup (90 g) sautéed asparagus and 3/4 cup (85 g) cauliflower rice. Total carbs: 7.7 g
Total carbohydrates for the day: 40.6 g

Wednesday
Breakfast: breakfast dish with 2 bulk firm-boiled eggs, 1 tomato, and 1 cup cubed avocado. Total carbs: 19 g

Lunch: 2.5 cups (244 g) shrimp garden salad with shrimp, lettuce, eggs, tomato, and carrots, with 2 tablespoons

(tbsp), or 30 milliliters (mL), olive oil vinaigrette. Total carbs: 10.5 g

Dinner: 3 oz (85 g) grilled chicken with 1/2 cup (78 g) roasted Brussels sprouts and 1/2 cup (93 g) boiled quinoa. Total carbs: 25.2 g

Total carbohydrates for the day: 54.7 g

Thursday
Breakfast: chia pudding with 7 oz (200 g) plain Greek yogurt, 1/2 cup (61.5 g) raspberries, and 1 oz (28 g) chia seeds. Total carbs: 27.1 g

Lunch: 1 cup (113 g) sauteed cabbage flower, rice with mixed veggies and 3.5 ounces (100 g) fried tofu. Total carbs: 14.9 g

Dinner: 100 g stuffed bell peppers and 3 oz (100 g) mince beef, 1/4 cup (45 g) tomatoes, 1/4 cup (26 g) shredded Cheddar cheese, and 2 tbsp (24 g) sour cream. Total carbs: 8 g
Total carbohydrates for the day: 50 g

Friday

Breakfast: green milkshake and 1 cup (30 g) spinach, 1/2 cup (75 g) strawberries, 1/2 medium banana, 1 cup (244 mL) unsweetened almond milk, and 1 scoop whey protein. Total carbs: 26.9 g
Lunch: 3 oz (85 g) barbecue lamb slice and 1 cup (105 g) Greek salad and 2 tbsp (30 mL) olive oil vinaigrette. Total carbs: 8 g
Dinner: 1 cup (205 g) tuna variety and 3 cabbage cups. Total carbs: 22 g
Total carbohydrates for the day: 56.9 g

Saturday
Breakfast: omelet with 2 large eggs, 1/4 cup (45 g) tomatoes, and 1/2 cup (15 g) spinach. Total carbs: 3 g.

Lunch: stir-fry with 3 oz. (85 g) beef, 1/2 cup (78 g) broccoli, 1/2 cup (78 g) carrots, 1/2 cup (85 g) snow peas, and 2 tbsp (36 mL) soy sauces
Dinner: 3 oz. (88 g) turkey minced meat round, 1 cup (180 g) grilled zucchini, and 1/2 cup (79 g) prepared couscous. Total carbs: 25.4 g.
Total carbohydrates for the day: 48.4 g

Sunday

Breakfast: 2 large scrambled eggs with 2 slices bacon and 1 cup (110 g) cut apples. Total carbs: 16.3 g .
Lunch: 3 oz. (85 g) roasted chicken with 1/2 cup (79 g) herbed barley and 1 cup (118 g) boiled greens. Total carbs: 28.4 g.
Dinner: filled tortilla and 3/4 cup (85 g) broccoli flower rice, 1/2 cup (120 g) black beans, 1/2 cup (90 g) tomatoes, 2 tbsp (24 g) light sour cream, and 2 tbsp (32 g) pico de gallo. Total carbs: 30g
Total carbohydrates for the day: 75 g
Add abundant of low carb vegetables in your meals If your gold is to maintain below 50 g of carbs per day, there is room for plenty of veggies and one fruit each day.

Healthy low carb snacks

If you are famished between feeds here are some healthy, easy-to-prepare, low carb snacks that can fill you up:

A slice of fruit Greek yogurt

One or two hard-boiled egg

Carrots leftovers from the previous night, a handful of nuts, some cheese and pork.

Conclusion

With diabetes, your body doesn't create enough insulin or can't utilize it as well as it should. When there isn't enough insulin or cells stop responding to insulin, too much blood sugar lingers in your system. With time, it may create major fitness concerns, such as heart disease, vision loss, and renal illness.

Printed in Great Britain
by Amazon